MENUHIN'S
HOUSE
OF
MUSIC

Menuhin's

Text by Eric Fenby

Photographs by Nicholas Fisk

House of Music

An impression of the
Yehudi Menuhin School at Stoke d'Abernon Surrey England
with a foreword by Yehudi Menuhin

PRAEGER PUBLISHERS

New York · Washington

BOOKS THAT MATTER

Published in the United States of America in 1970
by Praeger Publishers, Inc., 111 Fourth Avenue,
New York, N.Y. 10003

Library of Congress Catalog Card Number: 70-122929

Printed in Great Britain

The book designed by John Harmer

Foreword
by
Yehudi
Menuhin

The world is perhaps kinder to performing musicians than it is to any other category of human beings. Because of the 'intangible' quality of music, it can co-exist alongside other tangible pursuits without apparent conflict. We and our work are interchangeably regarded with a benevolent indulgence, as if to say: 'he, or it, is quite harmless—leave it alone.'

Even in Russia, notorious for its fierce suppression and intolerance of writers, painters, and even composers—not to speak of the human being in general—musicians are at least allowed to play. The housewife may sing as she slaves at her daily chores, as may the roadman; the crushing burden of slavery never extinguished the Negro voice; music seems to *accompany* rather than to *condition* life. This is not true of any other noticeable activity (pure thinking is invisible)—painting, eating, writing, running: these interfere with or replace other occupations. Society suffers the other arts as intrusions for which time or space must be allotted, and in consequence judges them severely and critically.

Of course the musician and the serious music-lover concentrate completely and exclusively on the music they listen to, but the general attitude to music is very much as I describe. My father often read newspapers while I practised, interrupted only by some *false* note or *ugly* sound I might make.

This principle has reached such monstrous proportions as to allow piped music to be the noisy witness of almost all our activities or situations. When I was a child, these experiments were conducted only in very advanced cowsheds (at the model Don Alda farms in Toronto, Canada) where it has to be admitted that an increased milk supply was the distinct reaction of cows victimised by soothing classical music. I have a suspicion that if the object of our stealthy manipulators be that of the stimulation of the glandular secretions, then, however perversely, they succeed in my case, for I sense a distinct discharge of adrenalin into my blood when I sit in a plane strapped to an armchair helpless before a veritable cascade of musical syrup upon take-off. Pinioned like a Strasbourg goose, instead of having rich food stuffed down my gullet, I suffer sickening music rammed into my ears and the effect upon my liver is identical with that of the goose. I am sure the guardians of Hades lick their lips frequently now as these force-fattened souls (*âmes-grasses*) knock at their gates.

This all goes to explain why I was able, in this most *tolerant* of countries, to collect in the course of only some three years a sufficiently concerted effort to launch a music school for children between the ages of eight and sixteen, who I could be reasonably certain would make their career in music; and why the school itself took as its working model the Central School of Music in Moscow, the happiest place I found in that most *intolerant* of countries—Russia.

Let me say at once that in respect of the spirit of mutual aid and encouragement between colleagues, there can be no better example than that of the Russian musician. Of course our children are not geared to the intense do-or-die discipline of the Russians, but it is our conviction that given a few more years, we will evolve to a point where we will be providing well-rounded musicians commanding their chosen instrument and, we hope, having exercised their other faculties, both individually and socially of a high calibre.

Again it is the virtue of music that, as with a mother's love which embraces many children, the musician is not exclusive in his affections. He also knows that the more good music and good musicians there are functioning, the more they and their music are required.

But the reader may ask, why the school? He only knows music as an embellishment, as an innocuous and apparently spontaneous by-product. 'The violinist is born': so, however, may be the criminal. But neither would exist without those special circumstances and opportunities conducive to their development. Nor do I deny the originality and gusto—yes even the defiance—necessary to both pursuits. Some people could feel in fact, that a school for young musicians might prove only the thin end of the wedge to a school for graduate criminals, furnished with full degrees.

Again, music too is a way of life. Often unconventional, nonconformist, it is the expression of what the creature is at heart, and his music reveals to the listener what this listener is to himself at heart. Music is the naked heart, the naked soul, the naked intellect even—as in some X-ray which transpierces all outer layers, skins and shells. Perhaps that phenomenon so dear to my heart—the untutored gypsy fiddler—comes nearest to expressing in the wild this way of life.

However, for your musician, music is severally a science, an art and craft. Indeed he must be born with certain aptitudes, certain longings and certain needs: yet these are but the seeds. In the school, as in a nursery for plants, we try to provide the soil and the gardeners who will encourage it to be *itself*, to grow into its own best expression. We must guide not only fingers, but minds and hearts, for music is a way of being. I wanted the young people to know the musician's sense of fulfilment and joy that comes of this way of being. This charming book conveys a real sense of that joy. Could it convey as well the many sour sounds which mark the beginner's efforts on the violin, for instance, the incredulous reader might indeed raise his eyebrows at the word 'joy'. But then, only the musician knows that real joy, real satisfaction, is but the reward for unremitting, patient and concentrated effort; for the musician's exuberance is legendary, making him or her, within or without music, a valuable contribution to society.

So it is this thrill of discovery, the capacity for *astonishment and sensation*, the pride that follows on endurance—all these that we try to foster. At the school we paint, sing every day, dance once a week, grow vegetables and look after chickens and a donkey. A small enough outlay maybe towards that love of life which with all the tragi-comedy implicit in this statement constitutes a musician's daily bread.

Perhaps (always excepting the ones in Russia) there has been no music school of this type for the young until now because it had to wait for that very atmosphere of new thinking in terms of education that has evolved in the last years; and is beginning to consider such elusives as the precious sense of mystery, curiosity and delight, dormant in every child and to attempt to conserve these qualities as an essential part of the openness of the young mind—an encouragement of which renders it all the more receptive to the three R's. For one thing *is* certain: where music is taught without these considerations, it withers, just as do most of the conventionally taught subjects in the minds and hearts of the average schoolchild soon after the escape from school.

All attempts to educate must fain be full of mistakes and when one realises it is the growing child who suffers more than his teacher, it fills one with apprehension. But we at the school feel that if we face this fact with all humility and with an ever-readiness to adjust, the child, sensing this empirical approach, guides us himself and the errors are less fatal, the co-operation of spirit more certain and the joy of teaching a wonderful thing. Whatever these children turn out to be, great or good musicians, great or good teachers, we do have a hope that they will be great or good human beings.

YEHUDI MENUHIN

13

"When did you last have your nails cut? You must be able to feel the key with the flesh of the finger at the very tip."

A small boy, certainly no more than ten, pauses at the piano; he is practising a Two-part Invention by Bach.

"Yes, they are rather long!" he replies, looking up smiling.

"Then ask Mrs. Cavanagh to attend to them for you."

Nodding, he resumes, completely unruffled, his mentor standing motionless behind him, attentive, following every sound.

"Be careful, there, in the second bar; play more deeply into the keys and not on top of them! Yes, that's better . . . but there are lazy fingers in that figure in the left hand on the third beat of bar seven . . . steady . . . your balance . . . you're not listening enough!"

The boy starts again. Style and fluency combine in clear, confident execution. Yet he could not have reached the pedals had he tried. His intent expression and upright posture seem almost authoritative in bearing.

Who is this child, and what is he doing here in this bed-sitting room in the heart of the country?

From a room further along the landing a girl, about thirteen or so, is working at an awkward passage from a movement of an unaccompanied violin sonata, also by Bach, an assistant teacher close beside her, super-vising her practice; watching her every action with the closest possible attention.

"Your intonation! . . . listen. . . . No, make the D sharp a little sharper! Lead in from the previous bar on the up bow. Good! . . . now, same with the G sharp . . . that's it!"

Again, the same intensity of purpose, the same rapt concentration as the boy's, in the far more personal involvement of finger and bow to string rather than finger and thumb to key. Here she is part of the sound she is forming within a hairs-breadth accuracy of pitch and, unlike the boy, supremely free from the readymade compromises left by the visiting piano-tuner. There is a musical quality in the shape of the phrasing; the child obviously feels and understands its content.

Two exceptional child instrumentalists, and both in the same establish-ment: surely this is remarkable?

But wait; a Bach chorale sounds from the room next door. Nothing unusual in that; until one observes that the child is sight-reading it at the piano in open score, admittedly a trifle slow in pace, but nevertheless reading from open score. That is, playing from four vocal parts simul-taneously, each part on a separate stave; but not only that: each part also in a different clef.

Passing along the corridors more instruments can be heard being practised with a thoroughness that proves expert teaching.

Then the unexpected happens: curiosity leads to surprise. Here in this extraordinary house of music, children are doing normal school work in class-rooms set apart outside. The classes are small, seven or eight children in each, and their studies range from English, History, Mathematics, Geography, General Science, to French and Art. There is something of the same deep attention here that marks their proficient, focused practising.

Eventually there is a break, and everybody makes for the dining-room. Thirty-six boys and girls collect over tea, fruit juice and biscuits in a great crescendo of chatter and laughter. Our three young instrumentalists who but minutes ago had seemed removed from earthly things, lost in the precisions of a mysterious art, are now no more than healthy youngsters indistinguishable from the rest, and ready to throw a ball about on the lawn. There are no compulsory or organised games at the school: the children improvise their own games as they please.

The age-bracket, one would think, must present some awkward administrative problems ranging, as it does, from seven to sixteen. Four timetables run concurrently to serve their various stages of advancement and make the fullest possible use of specialist staff and accommodation. The general impression is of extraordinary freedom within a discipline accepted reciprocally by all.

This break must be particularly welcome on three mornings a week at least when, for twenty minutes preceding it, the whole school engages in physical exercises away from their instruments. Then, after ten minutes relaxation, they are all back at work again. The four groups now interchange; those who were at school seek empty rooms and take up their instrumental practice; the others, including our former young seraphs, change to school-work for two forty-minute periods. Lunch follows with teachers and pupils in that gay and amusing companionship which music always brings.

Then, as if by magic, every young person disappears, and, incredibly, all is quiet. This, one discovers, in strict observance of a compulsory rule that requires all pupils to rest on their beds for twenty minutes each day after lunch.

New faces appear—some well known in the world of music—and for the next hour the children are free for one of their specialist lessons each week, whilst the alternation between school and supervised practice continues throughout the afternoon.

This is no soft-option school. Group activities for all children begin at seven o'clock each morning: for those of twelve and over—once or twice a week—as early as half past six!

These consist in the exercise of the basic elements of general musicianship: musical dictation; keyboard harmony and written harmony. But why at this unearthly hour? We shall discuss this later.

For some there are silent disciplines helping the mind to resolve such discords as the day may bring. Those pupils already stirred by the promptings of the soul may find such instructions in Yoga; a discipline unusual in an English school, but one which Menuhin has found enriching. There is no compulsion here, need one add.

After breakfast, for twenty minutes before nine o'clock each morning every one attends a class in solfège. Again, one might reasonably ask, why?

Supper is taken in the early evening when music and school may be forgotten in tennis, acting, dancing and handwork. There is pottery, too, and a lot of enthusiasm for building new cars from parts dismantled from decrepit old crocks on the benches of the school workshop.

Music itself, within its art, likewise holds surpassing pleasure even for those who have spent long hours in its technical service during the day. As soon as the young aspirants are judged to be ready, they may join with others in playing duets, trios, piano or string quartets, or share a back desk in the chamber orchestra. Nor are these pleasures confined to instruments in a school devoted to their practice.

Two weekly sessions in choral singing in works that span the ages from the sixteenth century Italian, Monteverdi, to the twentieth century Hungarian, Kódaly, accustom the children readily to the styles of those

composers who might otherwise be but names in their study of music history.

The fruits of these pleasurable music-makings are often of high quali and sometimes remarkable when art has become pleasure and pleasu art.

Here is a girl, a violinist of thirteen, playing in the manner born, wi style, confidence and verve, timing each musical inflection to a nicety warm, singing tone. Her violin is poised as if growing from her nec her bow, but a natural extension to her arm; her left-hand fingers faultless intonation—a model of her teacher's skill. She is being accor panied at the piano by a Chinese boy, perhaps a little older than sh with an artistry no less mature. He is punctual at every point of emphas and musical in every detail, lost and at one with her in the delicate lyricis of the Czech composer Suk's "Quasi Ballata", with an immediate gra of its challenging counter-rhythms—varied in sustained tensions betwee the players, both in superb ease of mastery so obviously within the powers; both rapt in enjoyment of the music.

Abruptly one realises one is judging their performances by standards the professional concert-platform, and not of school children just enterir their teens. This is a mystery beyond our knowing which brings embarrassingly near to tears. We are caught up in Traherne's mystic gaze of Felicity remembered through the eyes of a child.

'The corn was orient and immortal wheat, which never was reape nor was ever sown. I thought it had stood from everlasting to everlasting. Boys and girls tumbling in the street, and playing, were like movir jewels. I knew not that they were born or should die; . . . somethir infinite behind everything appeared which talked with my expectation ar moved my desire.'

Sounds of tuning from a nearby room snap the thread of reverie, ar arouse one's further curiosity.

The parts of Beethoven's String Quartet Op. 18 No. 4 in C minor a being put out on the music stands. Three boys and a girl, aged fourtee to seventeen, are about to rehearse the first movement. The viola playe the youngest of the four, surely was practising the violin previously! It no mean feat in a fourteen year old to adjust the left-hand spacings fingers to the larger fingerboard of the viola, play accurately in tune, a read his part in a different clef in music of this calibre.

Ten inches by three-quarters by five-eighths of an inch; that is th platform which really matters to any violinist worthy of the name. In th restricted area the four fingers of the left hand, supported by the thum

move freely within definite positions of the hand producing the notes in spacings that become progressively narrower towards the higher registers of each string. There are no frets as on the guitar to mark the exact places. An infinitesimal degree of error between the spacings of the fingertips renders the intonation false, hence the importance of the ear.

Chattering and tuning cease. There is a momentary pause while unity is established between them in quietness before beginning. All eyes are on the leader anticipating his entry—one beat before their own.

His opening phrase sets the mood and the music climbs into action with a fine sense of shape and purpose, and feeling for the operative note in each successive melodic curve. Ensemble is good, the design clear, and the phrasing pointed and unhurried until a quick passage upsets the rhythm where sixteen notes are meant to be played within one slow stroke of the bow. A sudden impetuosity: and the effect is as of stumbling into the next musical paragraph. An adult voice intervenes: a halt is called; the point is made and taken; the players try again.

Later the chamber orchestra meets to rehearse a Hindemith Suite for strings. Others, too, formerly at violin practice are now seen tuning in the viola section, and the remarkable young Chinese accompanist takes his seat among the first violins. Such range of instrumental skills in a boy so obviously accomplished, and still in his early teens, reveals what it means to be really gifted in the imponderable ways of music.

The Hindemith work is a cunning choice. Its firm, sinuous, athletic lines draw full, rounded tone from the youngsters; a lustrous sound belying their years. There is not a hint of a passenger; each player totally involved in response to the conductor's beat. . . . A hand-cla and the players are pulled up. "Well, some of us were good that time unfortunately, it's a unison passage!" An adult quip the children relish.

All members of this amazing family of young musicians retire betwee eight and nine-thirty, bed-times depending on age; lights are out—c should be out—half an hour later.

Activities, both musical and scholastic, cease for all at one o'clock o Saturdays. Those who live within easy distance may go home if the choose.

The most significant event of the week, whether the children ar conscious of it or not, is the recital or concert given by the music staf or visiting musicians of renown. This constant familiarity with musica excellence carries them forward from week to week, sustaining them b example in their own efforts towards their ultimate goal.

Thus, music is seen for what it is; an intrinsic part of the culture c man, an endless source of joy.

Mingling with this passionate apprenticeship are incongruous reminde of every-day life; the pin-ups and pop stars on bedroom walls; the para phernalia of the classrooms—a riot of children's paintings in rows, th smell of chalk, the botany-table; the extreme tidiness of the cloakroo with pegs all neatly labelled with names; the strange duality of life mirrore in the children's faces the instant they handle their instruments; th mini-skirts and jeans and Beethoven. . . .

Who are these children, and why are they here? Why do they give s much time to music when others their age are in school all day, and eve take school-work home at night? These are questions that must b answered.

Interlude
one

Catherine
Stevens
aged 15

Q: *How long have you been here?*
A: I've been here since I was eleven—that's four years.

Q: *I suppose you were selected from hundreds —if not thousands—weren't you?*
A: Well I suppose so, but when I was chosen there weren't quite so many who applied.

Q: *Have you learnt a lot do you think?*
A: A terrific amount, yes.

Q: *Progressing each term?*
A: I hope so. Of course, some terms I feel as though I'm progressing more than others.

Q: *Do you occasionally become disheartened?*
A: Oh yes. . . . I often think my standard is lower than the other pupils. I often feel that. And then other times it's perfectly OK—that's usually when I'm making more progress.

Q: *You have a lot of supervised practice here. Do you discuss your progress with your music master?*
A: Not really. One gets on with doing it.

Q: *Are your parents musical?*
A: Yes. My father's head of composition at the Royal College of Music, and my mother is a violin teacher. She taught me until I came here.

Q: *Is that why you're so self-critical do you think?*
A: Yes I think it probably is. My parents always used to sit with me while I practised. When I was little I was so self-critical it took me hours to do anything; but of course as I got older I began to be more independent in my practice. But I've found it certainly helps having competitors.

Q: *So you feel that this school has helped you much more than a more conservative type of musical education?*
A: Yes, I think so. I've been able to meet all sorts of people and discover about all sorts of music. Recently I joined the Essex Youth Orchestra and I do concerts with them a lot. We're going to Bath this week-end, actually.

Q: *To the festival?*
A: Yes, we've been invited by Mr. Menuhin to give a concert there.

Q: *Tell me about Mr. Menuhin.*
A: Well, he's worked out this system of exercises which he originally applied to himself. And he's given them to us. It's based on relaxation, and the tension is built up. I mean obviously one has got to be able to differentiate between tension and relaxation or else one would never get any intense feeling—but to be able to relax again after one has tensed slightly. Reducing tension to the absolute minimum you see.

Q: *In your playing do you try to strike a balance between technique and interpretation?*
A: Yes, very much. At a lot of schools technique and music are completely divorced. I don't agree with this, because when one has achieved a certain amount of technique this has to serve one's musical requirements. For example, on starting a piece ideally one thinks of interpretation—what is required musically . . . I feel I have to get acquainted with the notes first yet all the while thinking of what I want to do musically.

Q: *So far we've been talking only about playing an instrument and playing a piece of music which is somebody else's piece of music. Do you want to make your own music? to compose?*
A: I have tried—I'd love to compose. I don't get much time for it actually, but I'm hoping later that I shall be able to do that. I have composed a few things, outlandish compositions. I started a thing for about four horns and two trumpets, and another thing for xylophone.

Q: *What's going to happen to you personally in five years time? What are you going to be?*
A: I'd like to be a chamber music player. And teach.

Q: *How many of your friends here want to teach?*
A: Very few.

Q: *They want to do what?*
A: Well, some of them want to do solo work and chamber music but I consider that Mr. Menuhin has given us such a lot. His system of exercises is so marvellous —it's done me so much good, and I've studied it with my mother and it's helped her so much—and her pupils— that I feel, apart from anything else, it's my duty to hand it on to the next generation because it would be terrible if we just left it there and didn't carry it on.

David Holst aged 15

I am fifteen years old, and I have been here since the school started.

Q: *What instrument are you studying?*
A: I play the piano.

Q: *Presumably you had been playing for some time before you came to the Menuhin School?*
A: I heard lots of music when I was little, and I grew fond of music and was encouraged to play, so I started learning.

Q: *Your parents encouraged you?*
A: Yes. The initiative came from me, but then they encouraged me to play and it went on from there.

Q: *Are they musical?*
A: Well my mother was training to be a concert pianist but it never worked out. She was quite good, she played at two or three concerts, but she gave it up. My father can play the piano.

Q: *So that you grew up in a home where music was more or less taken for granted? Do you find, when you're at home that you tend to practise less?*
A: No. I think I practise—I wouldn't say more—but I practise about the same amount, and probably better because I haven't got other things to do.

Q: *Of course you have to divide your time at school between music and general studies.*
A: Yes, but I find I still have a lot of time to concentrate here, which is lucky.

Q: *Do you aim to become a concert pianist?*
A: If I'm good enough by the time I leave . . . it would depend on whether I go on to college. I'm hoping I'll be good enough . . . of course my main trouble is nerves. I'm terribly nervous when I have to play.

Q: *How do you combat this?*
A: I haven't really found any way of combating it except by trying to keep calm, and not letting myself get too excited before I play.

Q: *Do you find you become more relaxed after you've been playing a few minutes?*
A: I never feel relaxed, no. I find my playing gets a bit easier, but I'm still very nervous . . . even when I finish I'm nervous . . . I believe that Heifetz all through his life was terribly nervous when he was playing. . . . I think I'm better now than I was, and also when you're very young you don't feel the

responsibility so much . . . and I think if you've always been brought up to play in front of people, like child prodigies, you may get used to it. . . .

Q: *This perhaps raises the question whether there is a 'right' age for a child to start a concert career: what does your father feel about it?*
A: He wouldn't mind my giving an occasional concert.

Q: *In fact, there are more than 30 of you here at Stoke d'Abernon, who are all pursuing what one might call a musical apprentice-ship.*
A: Yes. Basically we are pursuing the same end. But there are so many directions. I mean, there is so much you can do in music.

Q: *Do you find when you play in the school orchestra there is a corporate spirit produced by all playing together?*
A: It depends very much on the mood the people are in, and the piece, and how the people are playing. I think one of the troubles with our orchestra is that it's too much like 19 individuals and not one complete thing, and I suppose we're slightly badly balanced as well.

Q: *Too many violins?*
A: Yes, as a string orchestra we're very top heavy. Of course, we could be very heavy bass-wise. We could play a few more cellos if we needed to. But this isn't what we need. We're rather short of violas . . . there's a tremendous lack of people wanting to play the viola . . .

Q: *If you weren't studying music, is there any other thing that you would want to do?*
A: Well, my father's in business and I wouldn't mind going into business, into an office. I'm quite keen on economics. I would never have minded this, and if I had to I still wouldn't mind, but I prefer music.

Q: *To return for a moment, if we may, to the nerves you spoke about earlier. Don't you find that your friends here have very much the same problem?*
A: Some of them do. Some don't. There are some people who are over-confident. Probably if you play well it's not over-confidence, I suppose. Let's say very confident. Some play well and some don't—and the same with people who are nervous.

Q: *Don't you think that nerves can sometimes be caused by hyper-sensitivity? And that possibly the hyper-sensitive person is a better musician?*

A: Maybe, yes. I think the best musician is a self-critical musician . . . somebody who, after he has played, can analyse what he has done and pick out the good things and the bad things. . . . I do know when I've played well and when I haven't, definitely; and I'm never put off by people saying, "Oh, you played marvellously" or "It wasn't very good". I know how I've played. If people say "that was marvellous, you played very well" and I think I didn't, it doesn't please me in the least to hear it.

Q: *And if you've played well?*

A: . . . I find that very gratifying . . . the trouble is people are so careful what they say after a concert. I mean they're quite ready to congratulate. They're not quite so ready to say "that was awful", which is a pity in a way . . . what I find worst is if people don't say a thing, because that's sort of middle plane. I hate people to be undecided.

Q: *Don't you find, after you've played some particularly difficult piece that you're excited and want to go on playing?*

A: Very rarely. If I've played well I'm thankful it's over. But if I haven't played well, I think, 'I wish I could play it again'.

Our English educational system conceals no more improbable unit than the Yehudi Menuhin School near London. Visitors are directed to make for Cobham some twenty miles south on the Surrey side. Cobham is now no more than a link with suburbia and the open countryside where a lane leads out to Stoke d'Abernon, a mile or so beyond. A drive appears unexpectedly, which winds through wooded parkland till the gable end of a Victorian villa is glimpsed through great trees which flank the approach on either hand.

In this place a dream has come true through the vision and resourcefulness of one man, embodying his ideals and passionate convictions in a school that bears his honoured name.

What, then, is so singular about his school and what, specifically, is its aim?

The answer is exciting to most musicians if disturbing to educationists. Here at Stoke d'Abernon, for the first time in Great Britain, provision has been made for the instruction of children of natural musical endowment enabling them to live together as a family in a fully professional musical environment, and specialise in music from the age of ten under a carefully selected staff of experts, yet combining with the statutory educational requirements.

The nearest approach to Menuhin's project is the traditional Engli
Cathedral Choir School where a seven year old boy may receive
excellent musical training along with his normal school curriculum ur
his voice breaks.

Menuhin's aim, characteristically, is simple and practical; to provi
the means for musically gifted children at that early age, paramount
their development and to run parallel with their scholastic education
as not to conflict with it; the ultimate aim being to produce by su
means either first-rate teachers or, in those whose character and gifts a
consonant with such opportunities, a further career on the concert pla
form. By tackling the pyramid of bad teaching at its base through increasi
the number of fine teachers of beginners, gradually—it is Menuhin's fi
belief—the base of the pyramid will contract as the effects of good teachi
rise to the top. This is not to say that a child of unusual talent will
discouraged from becoming an instrumentalist of the highest order.

A pertinent issue is raised at once upon which opinion is sharp
divided: the age at which specialisation should begin.

Educationists maintain that the education of a child should proceed
comprehensive lines and not until the later teens should specialisation
given full rein.

Menuhin and other eminent musicians, whilst supporting the need i
this broad inculcation, affirm that music is exceptional, and quite unli
all other subjects in the demands it makes to achieve its mastery; th
the foundation of a completely assured technique is dependent not o1

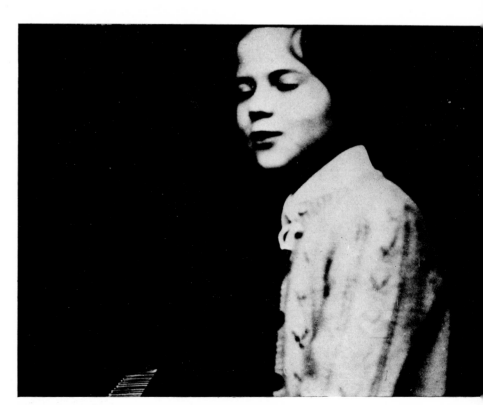

on sound instruction from the first lesson in early childhood, but on ho[u]
of supervised practice daily in aiming at that hard attainment. This, fr[o]
experience, is unquestionably true of those who venture their skill
strings. Wind instruments are essentially easier to play in the physi
co-ordinations requisite, and pose a different set of problems. Su
instruments have even been mastered from scratch when students enter[i]
colleges of music have taken them up as second studies: it is unhe[a]
of on the violin. Sustained progress to an advanced degree on the vio[l]
viola or violoncello is as much a matter of muscular development of [t]
child—in the same way as Olympic swimmers and centre-court ten
players are coached to develop the correct muscles from early childho[o]
The hammer-like precision in flexibility of left-hand fingers stopping [t]
strings in accurate spacings of perfect intonation; the subtle nuances
tone in every conceivable pattern of sound; these are not won with[o]
sweat and tears and the daily grind of hours of practice no matter h
naturally gifted the player. The violin is the most cruel tyrant of all a
exacts a lifetime's servitude.

Profound ignorance exists at all levels as to what it takes to deve
rare gifts, especially in the sphere of music. In no other subject is [o]
offered so much uninformed information, or is it less desirable.

Benjamin Britten recalls his dismay when, on announcing his youth
intention to be a composer, he was asked what else he was going to
in life. Writing a page of orchestral full-score would alone be enou
to daunt most people, apart from the nervous strain involved in
mental and imaginative processes of composition.

Menuhin, in the light of his vast experience in every continent of
globe, knows that potential musical talent is realised best by meth[o]
other than those to which our prejudices have led us. That to place s[u]
talent with the less-gifted in the hope that the former will improve
latter is a deadly error of our times, and usually ends in the extinct
of talent.

Nor can one always detect a talent capable of being developed to
highest degree. A child of seemingly outstanding ability may wane
promise in its teens. The comparative rarity of such talent in the classro
situation may prompt a teacher to ascribe what to him seems remarka
musical potential in a child who is in no way uncommonly gifted. C
didates for the musical profession need more careful scrutiny. The f
of our musical institutions must bulge with the glowing testimonials
equally misguided headmasters and headmistresses, for scores of stude
arrive each year who barely manage to gain admittance. They find t
their skill as instrumentalists so keenly exhibited by their school at
annual speech-day celebrations avails them little when called upon

play before their intended professor. Most are at the end of their music resources when they enter into their final third year. Many are utter miserable in consequence. Most would have been so much better advis to have gone to an established College of Education and there take mus as a special course, with the object of teaching it as a school subje along with others in the general curriculum.

Although ideally *all* children should receive some musical education t

professional level must be reserved for the gifted and determined; to
much public money is now being wasted in subsidising mediocrity; th
time and energy of our finest teachers which should primarily converg
in developing to the full the undoubted talent of the naturally gifted ar
too often debased in the hopeless struggle of trying to make musicia
out of those blessed with but a smattering of talent. So long as our offici
schools of music are expected to justify their meagre existence by admittin
these cohorts of mediocrity, the genuine musical potential of our natic
will continue to be given short shift at the most, or even allowed to fer
for itself. Elgar remained deeply seared throughout life by the bitt
struggles of his unaided youth.

The first step to sanity is to make it clear to all head teachers, parent

and the young themselves, that the possession of an "A" level in Music in the General Certificate of Education is not a passport to the profession of music. There is no infallible touchstone to offer those to whom it is given the awful responsibility of advising the young in the choice of a career; but in music there are signs.

There is felicity about a child the moment it takes up an instrument in its hands and makes a good sound. That is the moment to seek advice of those skilled in divining such mysteries.

The musical child of great natural gifts is apt to drift in isolation. Nobody seems to know what to do with him. Either he is left to his own

49

devices, or is all too readily warped with conceit. There seems no need to practise at all to beat his less able school fellows, and the temptation to fake destroys his initiative as he enjoys his easy role in the limelight. Discipline and the habit of daily practice, and learning above all to practise to purpose, are not acquired without direction which parents are seldom able to give. Geographical isolation, too, takes its toll of potential power: in particular, those children not within reach of a good music school are in danger through lack of proper instruction at the vital stages of development.

Now, to Menuhin's eternal credit, the dangers of isolation are past for those who become pupils at his school. I have earlier described a typical day in the lives of children of different ages at Stoke d'Abernon; specialisation throughout their school-life is, to Menuhin, imperative.

Selection, understandably, is stiffly competitive. Pupils are received only after an audition and are judged on their musical talent and character (the matter is dealt with in detail earlier on). A few steps inside the porch and the sense of family feeling is uppermost. This really is home but yet a school. And the children behave as if at home, free from the tension usually induced between those who teach and those who are taught. A quite remarkable relationship is apparent, easy, straightforward and unforgettable.

It comes as no surprise, therefore, to read in the School brochure:

'The image by which we are guided is that of an enlarged family so that the day-to-day life and work of the place is shared between young and old. This also explains why there is no system of prefects and no school uniform. Responsibilities are real rather than contrived and no attempt is made to create any artificial relationship between the generations. The adults are *in loco parentis* and accept the authority and responsibility which this implies. Problems of organisation and discipline are dealt with as they arise at a weekly general meeting which everybody attends. On Sundays those who wish to go to a denominational service are encouraged to do so, while the rest take part in a meeting of worship in the school.' On the subject of school uniforms Menuhin, characteristically, says that it is rather in the care of instruments and in the related aesthetic requirements of eye and ear that uniformity is encouraged.

Someone upstairs is practising Brahms. One is aware that the Musical Director's critical ear is as much concerned in following this as with the gist of one's enquiries. Marcel Gazelle, of the Conservatoire of Ghent, is the ideal man to guide budding talents in the way that they should grow. Dedicated absolutely to his profession, he gives himself unsparingly in his teaching, expecting nothing but the best response; implanting disciplines where needed and imbuing confidence in all. Clearly he earns his pupils' trust and personal regard in return. He has long been a close friend of Menuhin and was his accompanist for many years travelling extensively abroad, sharing his interests in the problems of teaching, and the particular difficulties of children who attend normal schools and try to study music as well.

A further quotation is also apposite:

'In the spring of 1963 Mr. Menuhin asked Mr. Gazelle to go to Moscow to see how music schools providing general and musical education are organised and to find out if any Russian methods could be adapted for use in this country. In the autumn of 1963 the Yehudi Menuhin School was opened.'

The conception and birth of a famous school can never have been disclosed to the public with more cryptic understatement.

Temporary premises were found and accommodation was shared, thanks to the hospitality of Grace Cone, with the Arts Educational Trust. During this time Menuhin cast about for a permanent home which would be self-contained.

Eventually he acquired the property at Stoke d'Abernon, and the scho moved there in the autumn of 1964.

It is difficult to imagine a more perfect setting for the full realisatic of Menuhin's scheme. The children's joyous and immediate reaction mu have allayed any doubts their distinguished founder may have had as the wisdom of moving out of London.

Success or failure of the project hinged upon finding a progressi Headmaster completely at one with Menuhin's aims.

Antony Brackenbury, M.A. of Magdalene College, Cambridge, ar formerly a master at Bryanston School, was obviously the man for th difficult task. He understands musicians thoroughly and the peculi difficulties they face in their problems; he has an intense love of mus himself, and a balanced view of its place in our culture. His methods a in line with the best modern practice and the school is recognised efficient on the register of Independent Schools at the Department Education and Science.

It is a mistake to imagine that these gifted youngsters, though primari concerned with the craft of their instruments, are a bunch of dullards other subjects. On the contrary, there is every evidence of high intelligenc At the appropriate age, those who have stayed the course as musicians- and by no means all succeed in this—may take the usual examination the General Certificate of Education. County and City Education Committees are prepared increasingly to allocate grants towards t expenses of individual pupils. This is heartening and of vital importanc

The establishment consists of two main buildings, the Music House ar the White House, part of which is the Headmaster's home.

An excellent classroom teaching block has been further added recentl The girls and the younger boys have bed-sitting rooms on the first floc of the Music House, and the older boys in the White House. Most of thes rooms are single or double and one has four beds for four small boys. Housemother, Mrs. Cavanagh, lives in the Music House and the Matro Miss Neville, in the White House; other resident members of staff shar the life of both Houses. Meals are taken collectively in the dining-roon of the Music House which is equipped with a first-class kitchen. Simp basic foods only are used in cooking, i.e. fresh meat, fish and vegetable plenty of salads and brown bread, fresh fruit and cheese, as it is felt th processed and preserved foods are unsuitable to a balanced diet fc growing children.

It is agreeable to add that this house which was previously a centr of training for management executives in the industrial world is now th nation's focal point in the education of children showing unusual promis as instrumentalists.

By virtue of its comparative youth the influence of the Yehudi Menuhin School is still mainly potential. The evidence before us, however, suggests that Menuhin has probed to the root of the problem of training the young for a career in music. The need, as he sees it, for a school such as his, presupposes his dissatisfaction with the general facilities provided for that purpose in the educational system.

Music is a great mystery and its exercise a great craft: to the gifted it is also a great art. When mystery, craft and artistry are coequal, then is revealed its power to transport. The things of the spirit are not neglected, nor the inborn ways of artistry; but it is right that in dealing with the very young, emphasis is on the grounding in a firm, secure instrumental technique with no forcing of the inner life of the child. Menuhin's School is not a hothouse for rare musical blooms, but the ideal environment where selected saplings, skilfully tended, can grow naturally to fulfilment. His school is certainly not for idlers, no matter how young they be, and reflects the intensity of his own apprenticeship in preparing himself for the exacting demands of a career in professional music-making.

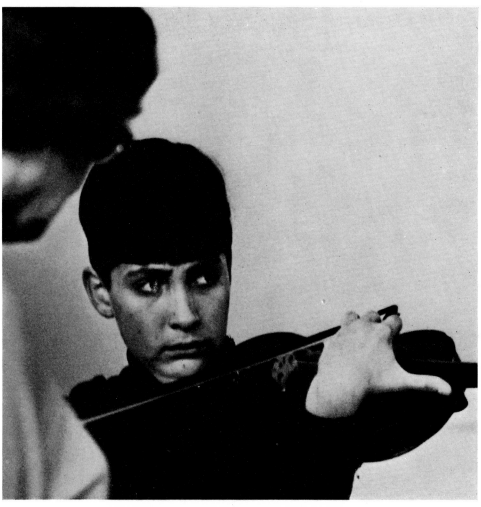

Menuhin's pupils are thus early at grips with the predicament whi[ch] faces all artists in all generations. Eliot's words* are equally true of [the] musician's task as of the writer's—

'. . . what there is to conquer
By strength and submission, has already been discovered
Once or twice, or several times, by men whom one cannot hope
To emulate—but there is no competition—
There is only the fight to recover what has been lost
And found and lost again and again: and now, under conditions
That seem unpropitious. But perhaps neither gain nor loss.
For us, there is only the trying. The rest is not our business.'

To help with the 'trying', every child is given two lessons each we[ek] from its principal instrumental teacher, each lasting an hour; plus a da[ily] two hours of supervised practice from a coach. Three and a half to f[our] and a half hours are spent each day on musical activity, depending on [the] pupil's age. But the child must first learn *how* to practise and, t[his] achieved, become established securely in the habit of *purposeful* practi[se]. The single most important factor in the musical function of the school [is] *supervised daily practice.*

Menuhin has obviously a great flair for attracting remarkable teach[ers] to his staff. His principal visiting violin teacher is Robert Masters, foun[der] of the Robert Masters String Quartet, who, as leader of Menuhi[n's]

* *Four Quartets*, Faber & Faber Ltd.

Chamber Orchestra, is a kindred spirit in artistry. Masters, a most cultivated musician, is a quiet man, kind yet authoritative and much liked by the children. Those who are his pupils are singularly fortunate, and doubly so if possessed of gifts to profit to the full. It is an essential and vital stimulus to the children to have such contacts as Robert Masters with the outer world of professionals.

Others who have been and are associated as teachers with Menuhin at this school—Frederick Grinke, Barbara Kerslake, Patrick Ireland of the Allegri Quartet, Christopher Bunting, Margaret Norris, Jacqueline Salomons and Rosemary Ellison—share his views and principles, and now Maurice Gendron, the distinguished French 'cellist, has taken over the 'cello section and makes regular visits from Paris.

Another regular visitor to the school and a close friend of Yehudi Menuhin for several years, prompts an anecdote:

Forty years ago I joined Delius, then a recluse through blindness and paralysis and needing my help to compose. He was living in a little village near Fontainebleau, which he had made his home. I would from time to

time escape from the routine and ride his old bicycle, through the forest, on the pretext of buying him oysters at Fontainebleau: Delius had a fancy for oysters like Mendelssohn for cherry pie.

My clattering wooden mudguards on the bumpy cobbled road compelled me to get off on entering the town and push the cycle till I came to the gates of the courtyard approach to the horse-shoe staircase on which, it is said, Napoleon abdicated. I was resting there over a pipe of tobacco on one of these excursions when I heard some accomplished piano-playing coming from the direction of the riding stables. My curiosity was further aroused on seeing a young American nearby with music under his arm.

Then one day, shortly afterwards, six young Americans turned up without warning at Delius's door. They were students at the American School of Music quartered, apparently, in a wing of the Chateau. Delius was unwell and unable to see them, so whilst his wife prepared some refreshments I was asked to show them the garden.

(contd. p. 73)

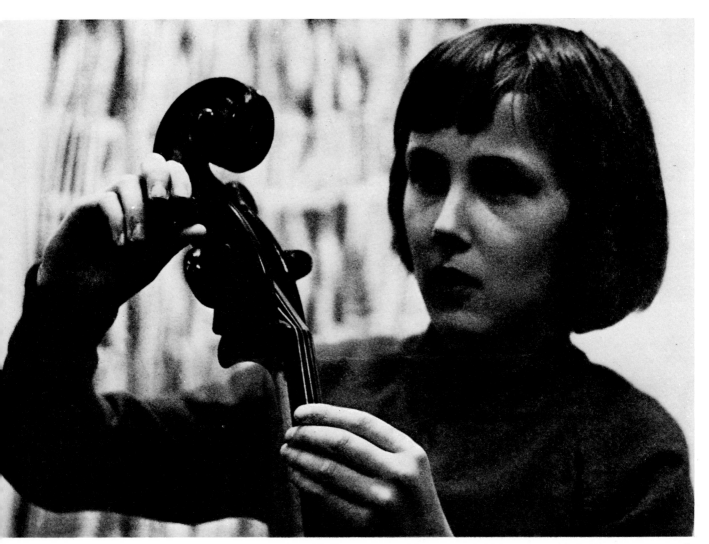

Interlude
two

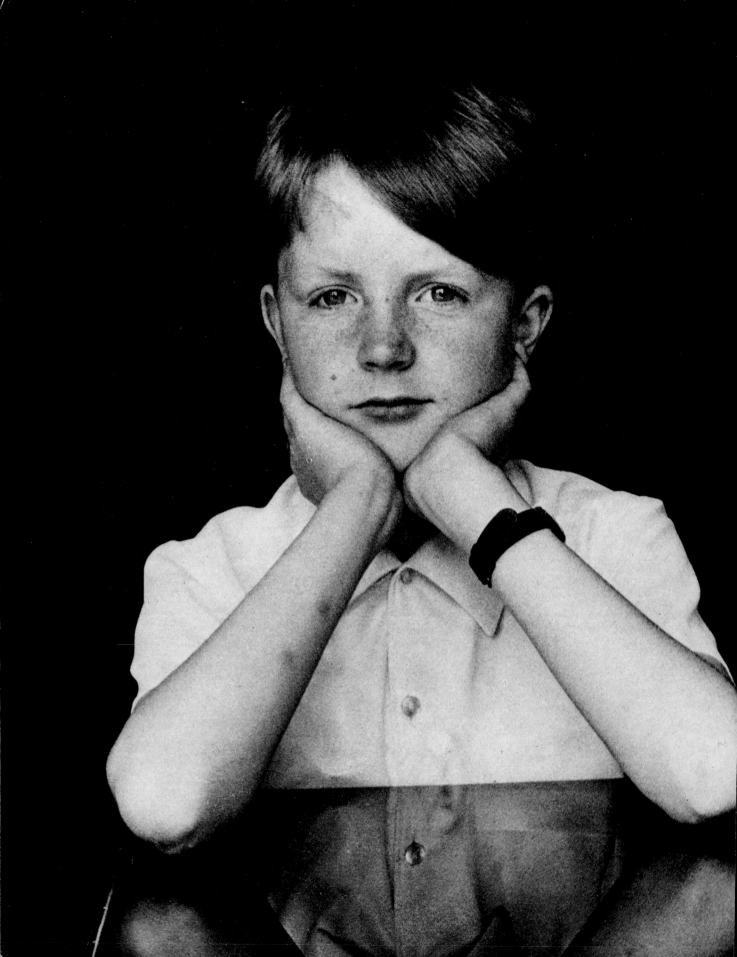

Simon
Parkin
aged 12

Q: *Simon, how were you selected to come here?*

A: Well, I went for an audition in February and then was eventually chosen out of a possible 240 candidates.

Q: *This audition was for the piano?*

A: Yes.

Q: *What do you particularly like about this school?*

A: I like the working atmosphere and the quietness.

Q: *Previously you were learning music, where?*

A: At a music school in Ormskirk, and before that in Liverpool.

Q: *Do you find it difficult to keep up your music in the holidays?*

A: Very difficult, with my three sisters playing around the house. But I try to keep a regular two hours a day practice; an hour in the morning and an hour in the afternoon. I tend to practise better after meals.

Q: *Can you remember when you first wanted to play the piano?*

A: When I was two years old. I first got to know a piano in the local baker's shop. And then my grandmother happened to have one.

Q: *Are your family musical?*

A: No. Only one side of my family is at all musical. . . .

Andrew
Watkinson
aged 14

Q: *How long have you been here now?*

A: This is my fourth year.

Q: *And how did you come to be selected for the school?*

A: Well, I played at the Glasgow music festival for three years and, largely as a result of that, later played for Mr. Menuhin when he came up for a concert. He said that he'd like me to go to the school as soon as possible.

Q: *When were you first aware of your interest in music?*

A: I think I've always been interested in music. I was encouraged to play the piano by my mother who is a pianist and violinist. I remember when I was six I was given some money for my birthday, and didn't know what to buy with it, so we went into Glasgow . . . and we saw this violin they were selling off and so I bought it . . . it was only a half size violin—at the time it was too big for me—and so I had to wait another year before I could begin; and then I had lessons with a very good teacher in Glasgow. I was absolutely terrified of her to begin with and cried at just about every lesson because she was so fierce and unkind, I thought. I'm very glad she was now.

Q: *Coming as you do from a musical background you don't need pressing to practise out of term?*

A: I try to keep it up for two hours a day, but there always seems so much to distract me at home.

Q: *Have you made any plans yet for your future when the time comes for you to leave the school?*

A: Well, I'm actually leaving this summer. I'm going to Dulwich College. . . . I find that I'm interested in a lot of things that I want to pursue.

Q: *Along with your musical studies?*

A: Yes. . . . I would like before I make a final decision as to making music my career, to have a chance to do other things . . . I'm pretty certain, ninety per cent certain, but I would like to do other things.

Q: *Such as?*

A: Something to do with mathematics probably. I find mathematics quite easy. My father and brother both studied engineering and mathematics.

Q: *Well, there is a kind of parallel between mathematics and music.*

A: It isn't a particularly popular subject all the same.

Q: *Won't it be difficult for you to study music as intensively when you're at Dulwich?*

A: I won't be able to practise for as long as I do here. But I'm going to study with Frederick Grinke, who did teach at the school the first two years I was here, and I hope it will continue.

Jonathan Rutherford aged 15

Q: *Will you tell me something about what you're doing here?*

A: I play the piano and compose. I'm taught theory by Mr. Weiss and learn the piano with Mr. Gazelle. Outside the school I'm having composition lessons with Lennox Berkeley.

Q: *Can you remember when you first wanted to play the piano?*

A: Well, I first started to play when I was in my pram. My parents had lots of classical records, and one particular Schubert song that my father put on I used to jump up and down in my pram as far as I could go . . . and they just thought I didn't mind music. We already had a piano.

Q: *Your parents are obviously musical?*

A: They enjoy music, but they don't play themselves: it goes back in the family. One of my mother's aunts used to compose pop songs. And on my father's side there's an organist.

Q: *Are you an only child?*

A: No. I have a brother who is two years younger. He plays the organ and piano.

Q: *Just now you mentioned having composition lessons; has your work here helped you in this respect?*

A: I think it has, yes. Learning how the parts in four-part harmony move makes my compositions sound more adult.

Q: *And this interests you more than a career as a concert pianist?*

A: Yes. But all composers, I think, should be able to play an instrument and think about giving instrumental recitals. It helps to make your name.

Q: *What sort of composition appeals to you most?*

A: Opera, mainly. I've written a short opera based on Oscar Wilde's 'Nightingale and the Rose'. I'm also writing some piano pieces and a small sonatina which is in $5/8$. But I hope to write another little opera to go as a twin to the 'Nightingale and the Rose', based on King Midas.

Q: *How often do you see Lennox Berkeley?*

A: Once every holiday, and at half-term.

Q: *Do you think that regular supervised practice helps?*

A: Yes, I don't think I'd have got so far if I hadn't been at this school. I probably wouldn't be so disciplined. I think that's the main thing I've learned here—and to set out my practice.

Q: *Is it a disciplined school in ways apart from music?*

A: In all the ways that affect our work, yes. But, I suppose, it is much freer than an ordinary school. There aren't so many rules. Quite often the children make up sensible rules that we hope the staff might approve of. We have a meeting every week and we decide things, and we all come to an agreement sooner or later and we try to carry it out.

Q: *Can you give me an example?*

A: Yes, bicycling on the lawn, and where we are allowed to bicycle. I mean, obviously it's not a good idea to bicycle on the lawn on a very wet day because it's going to make tyre marks and damage the lawn. Simple things like that —just to keep the school in good order, otherwise it could become a madhouse.

Q: *What would you miss most—apart from the music—if you were not at this school?*

A: The freeness, I think. But it's also the home life of this school I like.

Q: *Does the age gap between yourself and the younger children bother you?*

A: No, we all get on together really. . . . I just feel that we're all people. It's because it's so homely, I think, is why we get on so well.

Q: *And the fact that you're all musicians possibly helps? Do you play music together?*

A: Oh yes, there's quite a lot of chamber music. It's not organised, but you can go up to someone and say "would you like to try out this sonata or quintet, or something, with us, or me" . . . and everybody likes to do things with other people.

For the next half hour, as we sat by the river, they extolled the musicianship of Nadia Boulanger—regarded, they told me, throughout America as the greatest living teacher of music—and the prime reason for their coming to Fontainebleau.

"She's an incredible woman!" said one young man. "Her lessons are quite original; different and full of surprises. She quotes Valéry, and draws on painting and philosophy for . . ." "Yes," interrupted a charming girl "but, most of all, she shows one how to concentrate one's *deepest attention* on music; and how to awake in *others* a similar response to what

73

one is playing oneself."

It was this deep attention to whatever they were doing that stru[ck] me most forcibly about the children on my first visit to Menuhin's scho[ol]. Nadia Boulanger's influence is clear. The strictest disciplinarian herse[lf,] she never minces words even in her picturesque English. She loves [to] laugh: the children fear her, but adore her.

My story had an amusing sequel.

Later that summer the students wrote to Mrs. Delius offering to co[me] over from Fontainebleau and give her husband a concert. Delius agree[d,] after some persuasion, and instructed her to thank them and say t[hat] they could perform for him from his meadow: the meadow stretch[ing] beyond the far bank of the river at the foot of his garden, a considera[ble] distance away.

The music, of course, was barely audible from the house, and t[he] concert had started before Delius was aware of it. Mrs. Delius, whom [he] had forbidden to go, peered helplessly from an upstairs window whi[le] Delius, being read to by his German servant, dozed in his wheel-ch[air] below in the garden, and interrupted now and then to send the fellow [up] on the roof to report on the proceedings.

*   *   *

In fostering his pupils' deep attention to music, Menuhin has put fi[rst] things first; even to their place in the daily routine. Early in the morni[ng] when the child's mind is fresh, aural work begins, thus increasing t[he] mental perception of the inner ear in rhythm and pitch sense; that [is,] when the note sounded and the note thought—or known through memo[ry] —become one; or should become one through practice and intelligence.

The inner ear (as distinct from its medical meaning denoting t[he] complex and most inaccessible part of the hidden mechanism of the e[ar]) is a loose term used by musicians implying the aural sensory nerve-acti[on] by which musical sounds transmitted to the auditory cells of the bra[in] are analysed by the power of knowing through the habit of associati[on] or memory.

Its normal function lies in the world of external sounds, musical a[nd] non-musical, but fed by memory it continues to operate almost as vivi[dly] through the imagination in a silence independent of external sounds; [as] when a musician reads a score in quietness, or when we recall a tune in t[he] memory, or are cut off from external sounds when damage to the structu[re] of the outer or middle ears impedes the passage of sound-waves fro[m] reaching the inner ear, resulting in partial or total deafness, as wi[th] Beethoven.

It is a function we all possess, presumably, in varying degrees wheth[er] we can read music or not. Thousands go to symphony concerts or coll[ege]

gramophone records who are otherwise musically illiterate, a state which Frederick Delius preferred in a listener to that of technical knowledge.

Some, like the late Ivor Novello, compose and improvise at the piano by ear or, as the Beatles, similarly, on the guitar by ear, and have their compositions transcribed for them.

Other gifted people, however, as has already been implied, are able to translate sounds heard externally or imaginatively into exact musical notation wherein the link between the actual sound and its written symbol is perceived immediately.

At the Menuhin School, the children start their day writing down simple

tunes from dictation, or completing musical sentences spontaneously when the initial phrase is given them; learning to recognise the sound of chords within traditional styles and textures, and naming modulations of key encountered in actual music.

An alert perception of organised sound is the first essential to a professional musician. This is linked to knowing those sounds, just as we know our intimate friends. Once, of course, they were unknown to us until we were introduced to them. Eventually we recognise them at a glance; certainly without thinking. Exactly the same thing happens in music.

Any note at a given pitch has a character all its very own; to be recognised whatever its dress, whether it sounds through a violin, trombone, harp, guitar, or the human voice. When it moves to another note—and this it can do by step or leap—an immediate relationship is heard. These relationships heard from note to note have distinctive characteristics of sound to be loved each one for this very quality.

This loving of basic relationships of sound is the source of musical composition, and persists throughout a musician's lifetime. It is this that fires a child to compose because he is in love with these relationships. Left to himself, a gifted child, stirred by this love and imagination, ignorant of traditional behaviours in favour of this or that way in ordering the placing of sounds, will sometimes produce little pieces of his own— unusual and often quite bizarre. He may be for ever tinkering at the piano and earn his parents' misguided reproof; but the moment he tries to write what he hears, he then begins to outstrip his fellows.

The practical habit of thinking in sounds, encouraged by Menuhin
wise insistence, is exercised constantly outside school hours and, wh
knows, within them too with minds so young and full of music. Soun
are treated as part of their lives; there is no fear of them at all. They a
the natural effects of assured technique, to be transcribed in the min
whether written or not. The fear of sounds and contact with soun
certainly exists to an astounding degree in the majority of instrumentalist
Divorce them for a moment from the printed page and all their confiden
disappears. Play four chords on the piano; name the first, and ask wh
the last is, and they are completely stumped.

To come to a more apt and serious consideration. If, for instanc
whilst listening to a slow movement, say, by Haydn or Mozart, in a ke
already made known, for example, D major, if one were to stop the mus
suddenly and ask, "What key are we in now?"—pitiably few could tel
and even those may have guessed.

That is the problem that must be faced and which aural training h
failed to solve.

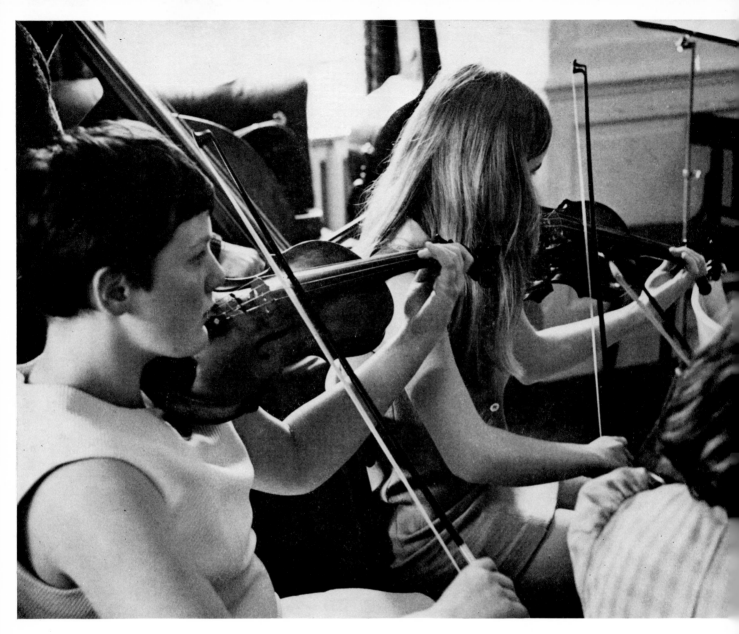

Peter Norris, to whom has been entrusted the task of assisting Marc Gazelle in alerting the aural perception of his pupils, is not only a fine musician himself, but one who understands their growing minds and shares their musical life with vision unconsciously lifting it to his own standards by guidance rather than precept.

The secret of Gazelle's work is his entirely musical approach. Proceeding from the simple premise—the sound first, its symbol next—the whole area of written work becomes an extension of aural perception in which the child finds satisfaction in absorbing and translating the ways of music almost without realising.

Great importance, however, is attached to attaining some fluency key-board harmony, another dreaded ordeal to most music students. This consists of playing chords, or inventing patterns based on chords

accompany a given melody with some regard to its style, structure, and shape when combined with pace.

Children sing their own written exercises copied out for each lesson. They are put on their mettle in sight-singing and learn what 'chording' means; they hear for themselves once and for all what is not immediately apparent to their ears on trying their harmony exercises on the piano—(because its similarity of tone tends to obliterate part-writing)—why certain relationships are crude and have been avoided by composers of sensitivity; why others lack balance; why the effect intended failed to 'come off' in performance; but most of all, they achieve a sense of line in shaping each individual part. This can all be done at the simplest stage with the simplest material by an imaginative teacher.

The Yehudi Menuhin School subscribes to these ideals with a minimum

use of the piano. Written exercises are adapted to pitches the children ca sing themselves, or the teacher supplies the bass himself. Each part mu be written on a separate stave and not, as is usual in text-book harmon with two parts to a stave, as though for the piano; a lazy way responsib for much bad part-writing.

It is my strong conviction that harmony is best taught in small grou of singers with a tuning-fork away from the piano; that is, taught creative through the vertical soundings from the free movement of parts which *counterpoint*, rather than from blocks of sound; in other words—wi emphasis on the *musical* approach from the very beginning.

A system of teaching is judged by results. One has but to ask a composer who has examined exercises in harmonic theory, to realise t effects of a method which reduces harmonic thought to formulae. Su ineptitude as is displayed by the student of average ability, whatever h aspirations in music, would not be tolerated elsewhere in any other bran of learning. Not a glimmer of artistry, taste or expression; nothing b mentally deaf deductions from so-called rules to find the 'right chord or missing notes in given chords like counting letters in a cross-wo puzzle. Such written inanities induce progressively a detestable paper-wo mentality which is the root cause of some of the worst music ever writte and the astonishing lack of harmonic sense, often quite elementary, many a skilled performer of today. Aural perception and the brain shou develop apace. It is the ear which is the sluggard. In correcting th dullness, the study of harmony should claim the attention of the *ear* first, the *mind*—second, and always—always of *pitch-memory*.

Again, how can the teaching of harmony be detached from guidance in taste? No distinction in taste is made between the often trite effect of a basic progression and its transformation into the musical poetry from which, after all, it is derived by the theorists. Lifelong adherence to such formulae without the power to transmute them into original music has stunted countless minds in the past.

The method of teaching harmony by imitating the styles of the great composers of the sixteenth, seventeenth, eighteenth and early nineteenth centuries as advocated by Dr. Paul Steinitz in his recently published book *Commonsense Harmony* (Mills Music Ltd, London)—based on the new (1966) syllabus for internal harmony examinations at the Royal Academy of Music—has more to commend it.

There is nothing new in this method. All great composers have taught themselves by studying real music and not from text-books; but they had the insight to know *what* to look for to help them in writing their own music. Elgar taught himself to compose by taking the designs of the G minor Symphony No. 40 by Mozart and inventing his own material based on Mozart's rhythmic and harmonic scheme.

One criticism, however, is that in completing set examples of real music of which one or two parts are given and the others are to be supplied, non-specialist students are often discouraged on comparing their first

miserable attempts at part-writing with that of the originals—which a
what they are *precisely* because of the *genius* of the composers.

Elgar's boyish method, of course, is more creative than that of Steinit
whose purpose is mainly academic.

Text-book harmony demands the capacity to think in four parts simu
taneously before the student can shape *one* musically. Dr. Steinitz begir
instead, with the completion of instrumental melodies from given fra
ments from individual composers. He then proceeds to two-part exercis
in the styles of Bach, Handel, Mozart and others in which the stude
contributes one part. This does not preclude work in free compositio
but the time factor invariably destroys this inclination in the vast majori
of students.

The chief difference here is that at the Yehudi Menuhin School the day-to-day method of teaching harmony is creative rather than imitative. Here feeling enters as through the fingers in drawing. As Chagall has said of the art of the lithographer, "there should emanate from each line a particular, spiritual quality that has nothing in common either with 'know-how' or with knack."

Learning to draw in lines of music—altering, improving, continually testing, judging always by the ear; checking the results in actual sounds, and doing it daily along with others as a perfectly natural activity in the reciprocal company of inspiring teachers—gives a child a supreme advantage in mastering the elements of the craft of music at an earlier age than would be possible attending a normal school. That is Menuhin's intention.

The staff enjoy freedom of action and are not hamstrung by examination requirements. Marcel Gazelle himself takes charge of solfège which embraces sight-singing, transposition, theory, harmony, and even musical history as introduced at Stoke d'Abernon. Solfège is a method of developing musicianship, used extensively in Belgium and France, by which the elements of melody, harmony, rhythm and tone are fused to promote literacy with aural perception (not necessarily developed in those who play an instrument with fixed notes like the piano).

The root of the matter is in solmization, the function of naming each note of the scale with a particular syllable in two systems: the fixed doh, which is always C, with other syllables related accordingly; the moveable doh which may be any note (also with other syllables related accordingly)

or as a temporary keynote of the moment caused by modulation. We come nearest to solfège in that small part of it used in England which is closely akin to our tonic sol-fa. The very mention of tonic sol-fa in the context of the Menuhin school must amaze those who remember with horror the ordeals of their schoolday experiences of the subject.

A recent pronouncement by a Minister of State that he hoped that schools would soon "get rid of all that nonsense of tonic sol-fa" concealed more truth than he realised.

As taught in our State Schools, with few exceptions, *it is nonsense*; a travesty of the real thing. It is not the system that is at fault, but the teaching of it that breaks down: and always at the decisive stage when translation to staff notation is attempted. When taught with imagination and skill it is in itself the most *accurate* method yet devised in learning to pitch the various steps and leaps between successive sounds which form in procession a melodic line.

The last President of the Tonic Sol-Fa College was none other than the late Sir Malcolm Sargent; this office was no sinecure to him. A high proportion of the amateur singers in the great choirs he conducted regularly rely *entirely* on tonic sol-fa to master the difficult modern works they are expected to perform in the repertoire of today. When in rehearsal an awkward interval continued to give trouble to those of his singers who were reading from staff notation, Sir Malcolm invariably corrected it in reverse by singing slowly the appropriate translation from staff notation to tonic sol-fa—if not already provided in the copy, a practice now growing with all music publishers.

Properly taught—and this is imperative—tonic sol-fa has an irreplac[able] practical purpose in the musical training of the young: solfège [as] revealed by Nadia Boulanger and Marcel Gazelle, *infinitely more so*. Y[et] even on the basis of sol-fa, how many students in our colleges of mus[ic] or departments of music in universities have a working command of t[he] system of clefs? The treble (G) clef and the bass (F) clef are familiar [to] most of them through their use in piano music: but it is not unusual [to] find a violin student unable to read the bass clef. When it comes to t[he] moveable C clef in either its alto position on the third line of the stave [as] it is to be found in music for viola, or in its tenor position on the four[th] line of the stave in music for violoncello, bassoon and trombone, confusi[on]

Interlude
three

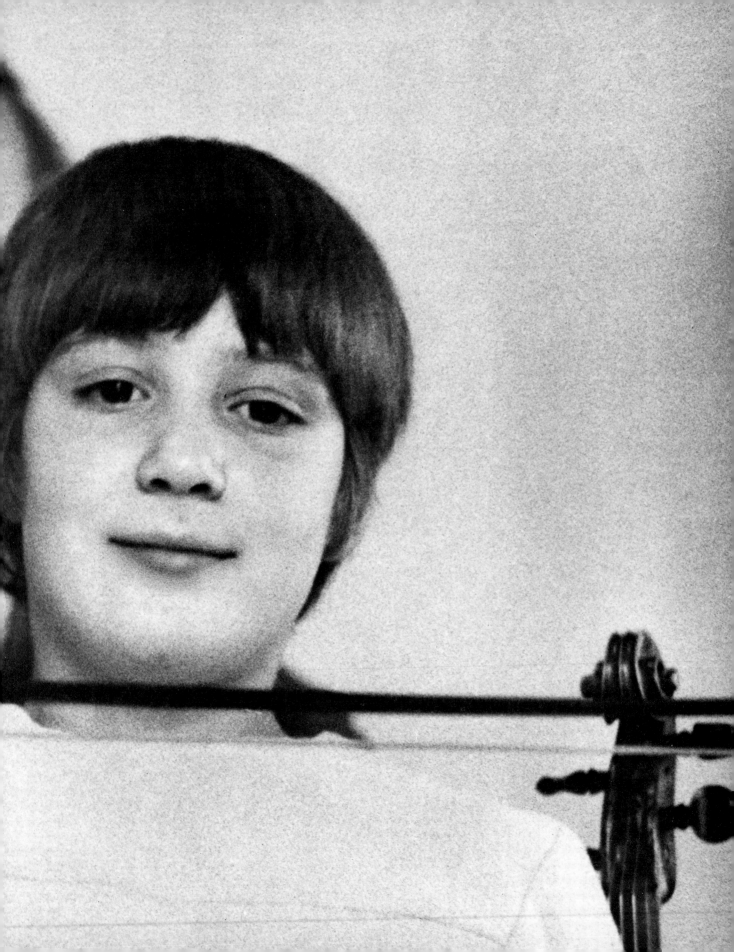

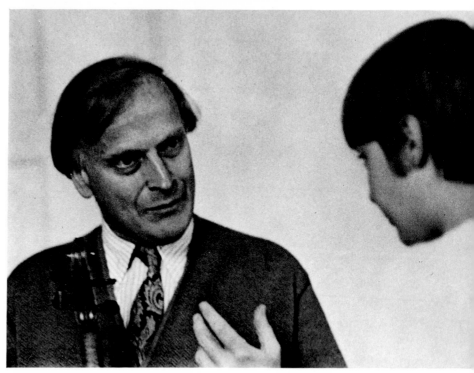

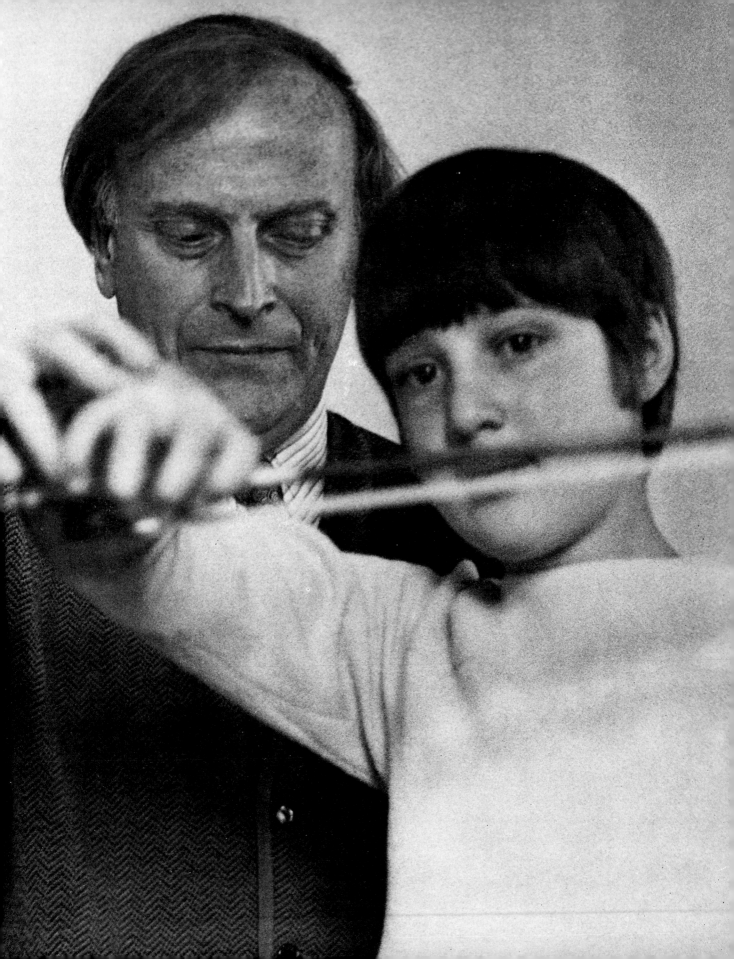

is worse confounded. Students reach the end of their courses barely able to read the C clef in its alto position in the string quartet score-reading tests which are required of them at the piano to pass certain examinations. Fluency is seldom met with, either, in the C clef in its tenor position; and knowledge of it in its soprano position on the first line of the stave, which is indispensable to a serious study of the vocal art of the Middle Ages, is a very rare accomplishment. This partial literacy could have been avoided in a firm grounding in tonic sol-fa in the Junior School by an expert teacher on the simple principle of the moveable doh.

Clefs present no problems to Marcel Gazelle's pupils. All music is an open book to them.

How does Menuhin select his pupils for entrance to the school? Wh.
are the criteria?

First, and foremost, there must be evidence of genuine talent for tl
violin, violoncello or piano and other instruments. This is certainly not ea:
to explain: instantly one is confronted with mystery. Why, for instanc
can one small child pick up a tin whistle and produce immediately
pleasing, accurate sound whereas another can only make it squeak? Anoth
tries a violin and straightaway makes a good sound whilst in yet another
hands it will only wheeze and groan. Whatever it is, knack or gift, tl
ability to make a good sound on a violin is imperative as a start. Similar
with a flair for the piano. Secondly, physical ability is insisted upo
Thirdly: there are ear tests. Fourthly: singing tests. And whatever Men
hin's own decision, there are still two crucial questions to be answere
Does the child want to come to the school of its own accord? Or is it sole
at the parents' wish?

The requirement of physical ability becomes clear; Menuhin's methc
of violin playing is based partly on a general physical condition of flexibilit
resilience and balance, of good breathing, which require a certain amou
of preparation (or practice) away from the instrument. Much of this i
of course, applicable also to the piano and on which Marcel Gazelle h
grafted specific pianistic requirements.

Dexterity is largely a matter of the right control of the right muscle
the strengthening of the fingers; the auxiliary function of the wrists ai
the weight of the arms in relation to the sound to be produced on keyboai
by fingers and thumbs, or on strings by fingers and bow. Two differe:
sets of problems, but both complementary. There are general exercises ai
those relating to particular uncertainties of technique. The unravelling ai

regulating of these tensions and relaxations unlock sources of hidden pow
in gradations of extreme subtlety. Awareness and the means of contr
of these forces are fundamental to progress.

Menuhin is deeply absorbed in his school, teaching there whenever
can between his strenuous concert tours. That an artist of such eminen
and world-wide fame should seek out children to communicate his know
ledge, and concern himself actively with the next generation of teache
seems quixotic, to say the least.

The children he accepts cannot all be exceptional. But whether th
become teachers, orchestral players or soloists, their influence must
for good and they will have earned the privilege of sharing an experien
unique in English musical education.

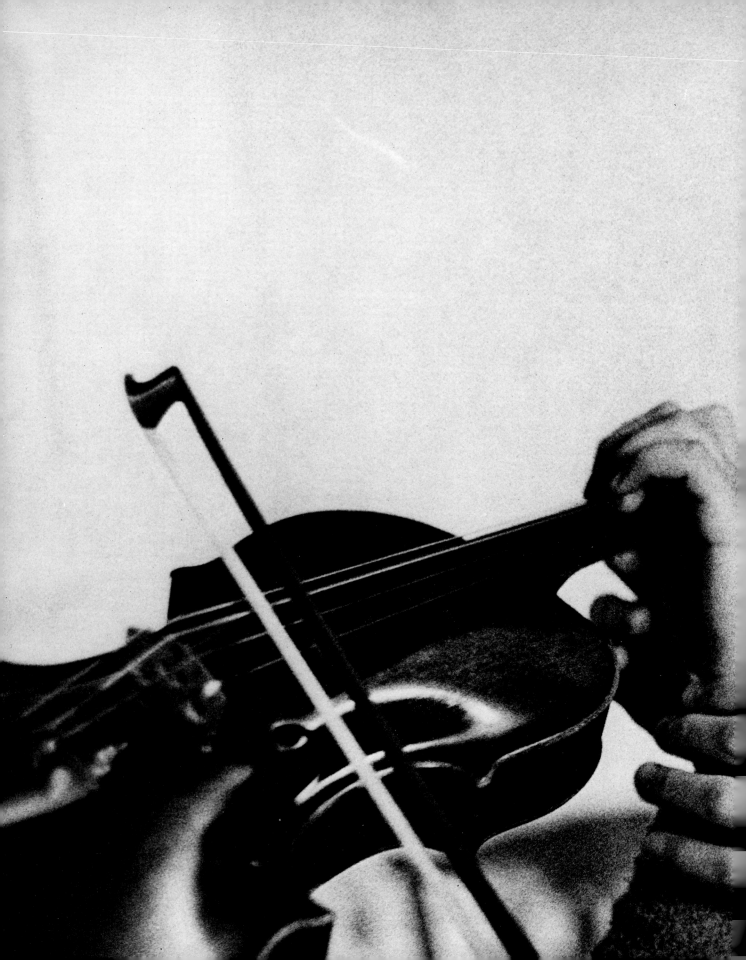

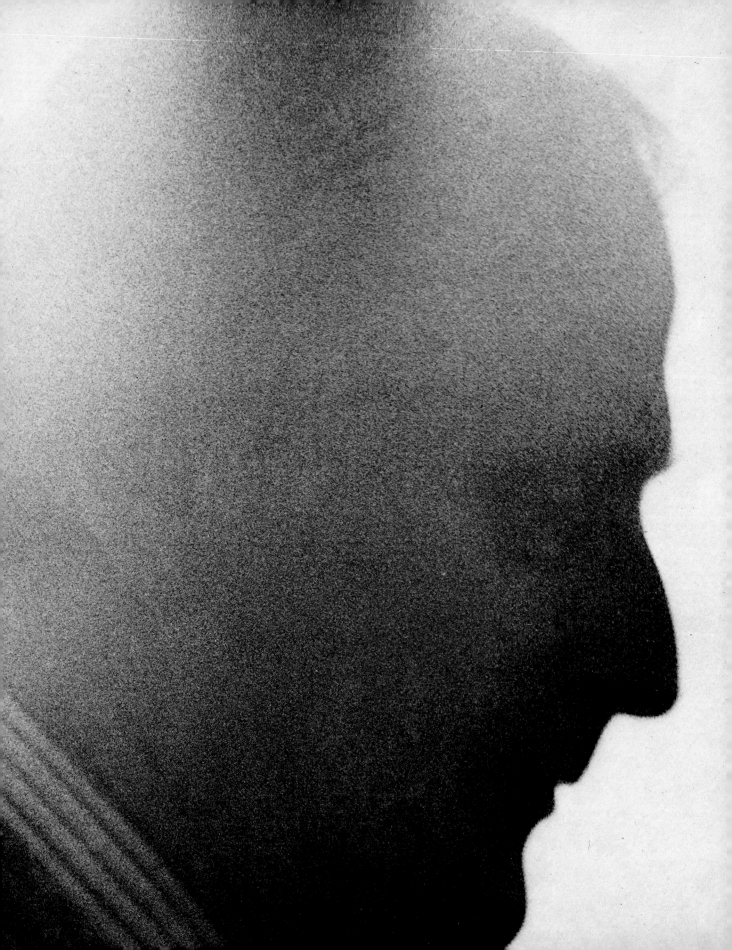

This may be the place to say something about the very great man who is living amongst us although of American birth and upbringing.

I remember that the first mention of the name Yehudi Menuhin made little impression in the characteristically insular English musical circles of the time. Yet Menuhin, at the age of 9 and 10, was already ravishing not only audiences but music critics in Paris, Berlin, New York, San Francisco and many other cities.

When, at last, he came to London in 1929 as a boy of 13 to play the Brahms concerto with Fritz Busch and the London Symphony Orchestra on 10th November, and followed this with a recital at the Royal Albert Hall with his accompanist, Hubert Giesen, press and public were spellbound in the presence of undoubted genius. Before leaving for a European tour Menuhin recorded his first concerto with orchestra—the Max Bruch conducted by Sir Landon Ronald.

An even greater triumph awaited Menuhin in London in 1932. Frederick Gaisberg of H.M.V. had set his heart on Menuhin's recording the Elgar concerto with the composer conducting. Harold Holt, the concert impresario, arranged for a public performance at the Royal Albert Hall on Sunday, 30th November. The occasion was unforgettable.

Menuhin was to play three concertos, by Bach, Mozart, and Elgar.

Elgar, then a revered figure who had just celebrated his seventy-fifth birthday, was to conduct his own work and Sir Thomas Beecham the others. Beecham, who detested musical prodigies, had needed no little persuasion from Holt to take part in the concert, as he afterwards confessed to me, but had relented on learning of Elgar's total suspension of disbelief that a boy still in his teens could play his music so perfectly. Music-lovers throughout the country were thrilled with expectation. No

wonder a ticket was regarded as a privilege and the vast hall sold out wee[k]
in advance. Representatives of the Royal Family were present together wi[th]
the Prime Minister and members of the Cabinet.

The moment the boy entered and made his way through the ranks of o[ur]
finest orchestral players, he completely dominated the scene; when [he]
began to play it was as if some celestial being had been sent to assure us [of]
our destiny. Not since Kreisler had such lyrical beauty of tone and phra[s]ing been heard in London. The violin in his hands seemed incapable [of]
even an instant's roughness, or the slightest unpleasantness of soun[d.]
Beecham who, at heart, never really enjoyed the secondary role of orche[s]tral accompanist, least of all in Bach, was obviously in his element. Eve[ry]
member of the audience knew that this was an afternoon in music th[at]
never could occur again: when the collective mind of the assembly w[as]
gathered up into "the stillness where our spirits walk" by a boy with [a]
violin.

Menuhin can have made no deeper impression in the whole of his distinguished career. From that moment onwards he was regarded with awe.

His feat in playing three difficult concertos at a single concert in company with foremost musicians seems barely credible in one so young. The grasp of such disparate works is amazing, the triumph of memory, the conquest of purely technical obstacles, rendered apparently with consummate ease, defies description of all that was involved. Many remarked on a quality of sound they could not remember having heard before, indefinable, but as of innocence that informed the more heart-searching melodic lines as seemingly only this child could do.

Then followed what must have been hard years for him in preservi
a balance between boyish inducements and the insatiable demands
the violin. His quota of concerts, regulated wisely, was free from paren
exploitation—he was then giving about twenty a year—but the boy's l
was circumscribed by his teacher's and immediate family environme
All decisions were made for him; even in his late teens social conta
were fleeting and few, and the protective screen was rarely lowered.

The transition to mature manhood brought Menuhin up against
crucial and what must certainly have been an alarming problem. Howev
good his teachers—and he has often acknowledged his indebtedness
them—the sheer perfection of his attainment before he had entered up
his teens can hardly be ascribed in full to their tuition, indeed to any ki
of tuition. A current of unfathomable intuition, maybe, had sustained t
security of his technical resource without his ever being able to explain
Gradually, for whatever reason it may have been, Menuhin found hims
experiencing the kind of agonising realisations that must haunt the liv
of all great virtuosi, and when he was twenty his parents organised a fami
retreat from public life for some eighteen months.

It was during this period that Menuhin realised how little he kne
that was communicable about his instrument, and teachable to othe
His pupils at Stoke d'Abernon represent therefore a real fulfilme
of a deep and lifelong urge—a two-pronged urge—to master and com
municate. This has now taken the shape of a logical and reveali
approach—one might say a comprehensive method, if one may use th
desiccating term totally at odds with the artistic impulse, which h
captured the imagination of his colleagues as well as the children at th

school. Of course it is understood that technical mastery is only a means towards gaining the interpretative imagination.

Menuhin as an artist is known as untiring in his relentless pursuit of absolute perfection in presenting music, in performance, with truth to its inner meaning and faithfulness to its style. His taste is both catholic and eclectic, embracing a love of all the arts with a deep feeling for and knowledge of the structural and aesthetic qualities of the music of Eastern countries. Whenever Menuhin plays in public the impression is of one fulfilling a high and noble function as a musician, and not performing merely to give pleasure to the listener. He never allows us to forget that the role of music is to transport.

Menuhin would agree with Maritain that men are united only by the spirit. He has said as much in his own words and the pattern of his own life of dedication and service. His school is a private institution and depends overwhelmingly on the generosity of individuals, although Foundations, the Arts Council and Educational Grants are contributing substantially.

Through the course of his friendships with leading musicians of all nations of the world he has sought to promote better understanding between people wherever he has gone and his name is linked with innumerable activities over a wide range of endeavour in the humanities, especially for those in want. One wonders he has any time for his music.

Something of the quality of Menuhin's mind may be gauged from remarks he made in his presidential address to the Incorporated Society of Musicians in 1965:

"When we work at a piece of music or perform it, our attitude is one of co-operation with, not resistance to, the music. As interpreters we are middlemen translating the composer to our listeners—we are therefore vessels which receive, hold, and release—at no point is there a loss or a blockage implied. Nor is this high function confined to the greatest music only.

"Now I do not want to stress the solemn at the expense of the earthy, the buoyant or even the vulgar. We need and want music of every description and musicians for every kind of music. We as musicians, performers and teachers, must explore beyond our routine duties to stimulate and enrich our sense of rhythm, of colours, our instrumental techniques, our teaching abilities . . . certain standards could be set—in training in instrumental techniques, particularly in string playing, in interpretation and style, which would give our young people a better start. Now that musicology has revealed so many hidden treasures; new materials for teaching should be drawn from all periods, as well as specific rhythmic and melodic exercises borrowed from other practices in music, other civilisations, and graded according to difficulty, from elementary to advanced and involved. Children should be stimulated to express themselves in music—music of their own making. We must reinstate the various ancient disciplines of improvisation, one of which survives on the organ today, others in jazz, to make music an integral part of a child's equipment. . . . We in those branches of dissemination—in teaching and performing parts—must not lag behind the instincts and the demands of the child."

We may be sure these convictions are being put into practice at the Yehudi Menuhin School.

The Publishers wish to express sincere thanks to Mr. Antony Brackenbury, Monsieur Marcel Gazelle and the staff and pupils of the Yehudi Menuhin School for their kindness and help during the production of this book.

Academic Staff

Headmaster: A. H. Brackenbury Esq., M.A.
Assistant Teachers: Miss D. Chamberlain, N.F.F.
G. M. Vaughan Esq., B.A.
Part-time Teachers: Mrs. J. Robinson, B.Sc.
Mrs. M. Trevelyan,
Slade Diploma of Fine Art

Music Staff

Music Director: M. Marcel Gazelle
Violin Teachers: Mr. Robert Masters
Mme. J. Gazelle
Mrs. Margaret Norris
Violin Supervisors: Miss Marcia Crayford
Miss Rosemary Ellison
Chamber Music and
Viola Teacher: Mr. Patrick Ireland
In charge of 'Cello classes: M. Maurice Gendron
Cello Teacher: Miss Myra Chahin
Cello Supervisor: Miss Audrey Tointon
Piano Teachers: M. Marcel Gazelle
Miss Barbara Kerslake
Piano Teacher/Supervisor: Mr. Joel Ryce
Piano Supervisor: Miss Yaltah Menuhin
General Music Subjects: Mr. Peter Norris
Dancing and Movement: Mrs. Janet King

Administrative Staff

Secretary: Mrs. Jena Morris
Housekeeper/Cook: Mrs. U. M. Cavanagh
Matron: Miss D. M. Nevitte

Mme. Nadia Boulanger visits the school regularly, and works with the pupils in groups and individually.

Yehudi Menuhin's first "Music Academy Committee" was formed som
five years ago in London with the help of the Marchioness of Cholmondele
The Marchesa Origo, The Lady Fermoy, The Countess of Straffor
Madame Gina Bachauer, the late Lord Mottistone, Mr. Paul Paget ar
others. Its object was the founding of a boarding school—the only one
its kind outside Russia—where unusually gifted children would recei
regular instrumental tuition and practice under expert guidance, combine
with a broad general education of high standard.

Thanks to Miss Grace Cone, a start was made in 1963 with 15 children
collaboration with the Arts Educational Trust. In 1964 the premises
Stoke d'Abernon were acquired. The school now has 36 resident pupi
and it is hoped to extend the existing premises to accommodate the eve
increasing number of talented young applicants.

The school has received official recognition from the Department
Education and Science but still remains a private school dependent o
the generosity of contributors from various sources sympathetic to its aim

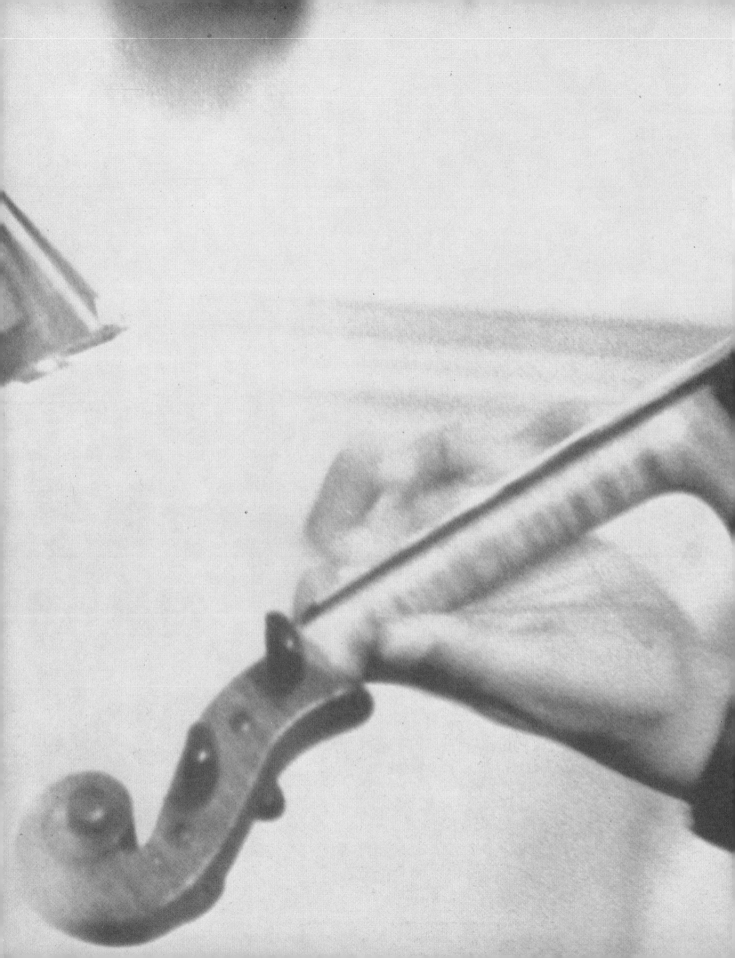